CAN I

with violence? Legally, do you have to wait for someone to strike first before you can defend yourself? What are the best techniques to use if your assailant is stronger and more skilled than you are? And what about defending against weapons and even gang attacks?

These are just some of the questions answered in *Self-Defence in 30 Seconds!* Drawing from more than two decades of extensive international experience — including providing close personal protection to aid workers in Iraq and teaching his own system of self-defence to the American FBI, the British SAS and Nelson Mandela's bodyguard team — Robert Redenbach provides proven strategies for protecting yourself and the people you care about.

www.redenbach.com

Also by Robert Redenbach
Waveman

SELF DEFENCE

SELF DEFENCE IN 30 SECONDS!

ROBERT REDENBACH

COURTNEY
BALLANTYNE

COURTNEY BALLANTYNE

Courtney Ballantyne Publishing
PO Box 201 Bond University
QLD 4229 Australia

First Edition September, 2007

Retail Distribution by
Macmillan Publishing Services
Level 1, 15-19 Claremont Street
South Yarra VIC 3141

National Library of Australia
Cataloguing-in-Publication data:

Redenbach, Robert P.
Self-Defence in 30 Seconds!

ISBN 978-0-9803822-0-4

1. Self-Defence. 2. Personal Security. 3. Defensive Tactics.

'Do the thing and you will have the power.'

Ralph Waldo Emerson

Contents

A Note to the Reader   1

1 *The Anatomy of Pressure*   3
  The Error
  The Bubble of Confusion
  The Result
2 *Fear*   9
3 *Confidence*   17
4 *Defence Assumptions*   23
  Your Opponent Is Under an Influence
  Your Opponent Is Armed
  Your Opponent Has Supporters
  Your Opponent Will Charge
  You Are Being Filmed
5 *Your Options*   29
  Ignore/Leave
  Comply
  Dominate
  Stun and Run
  Restrain
  Incapacitate
6 *Assegai*   37

Contents

7 *The Four-Flow Cycle*   41
   Shift Balance
   Shift Focus
   Seize Opportunity
   Compel Response
8 *Pre-Contact*   45
9 *Weapon Defence*   49
10 *Ground Defence*   53
11 *Multiple Defence*   57
12 *Fighting Fit*   61
13 *Train to Improve, Not to Impress*   75

Recommended Reading   77

A Note to the Reader

THERE ARE only two rules of self-defence: 1) avoidance and 2) survival.

Self-Defence in 30 Seconds! has been written for people with the maturity and good sense to appreciate the value of avoidance.

In a perfect world there would be no need for the second rule of self-defence.

Unfortunately, our world is not perfect and physical assault happens. If it does happen to you, you have the right to defend yourself. Similarly, if an aggressor attacks someone you care about or who is unable to protect themselves, you can help.

Unlike a boxing match or a martial arts competition, a physical assault does not involve willing participants whose aim is to accumulate points within a predetermined framework designed to prolong the event while simultaneously entertaining spectators.

In a real self-defence situation, once conflict becomes physical, you have, at best, 30 seconds to save yourself.

Unless you are a talented and highly trained athlete, it is a tactical error to believe that if you can't defend yourself in the first 30 seconds, *more* time in the affray is going to help. It won't.

1

It's like trying to save yourself from drowning; if you can't do what needs to be done in the first 30 seconds, *more* time in the water is going to make the situation worse, *not* better. With this in mind, I have written *Self-Defence in 30 Seconds!*

I've cut to the bone of what it takes to understand how to survive a violent encounter. The end result is deliberately brief as I've followed the maxim: *It's not daily increase, it's daily decrease; hack away at the non-essentials!*

It has taken me over two decades to 'hack away' the non-essentials of self-defence. During that time I've travelled to and worked in over thirty countries. Many of the insights gained from those travels are described in my autobiography *Waveman*.

The purpose of *Self-Defence in 30 Seconds!* is to take the experiences of *Waveman* and provide you, the reader, with an honest appreciation of what really matters when it comes to protecting yourself and the people you care about.

Travel well, and stay safe.

Robert Redenbach

1

The Anatomy of Pressure

HAVING TAUGHT the subject of self-defence to thousands of people, and given interviews to scores of journalists, I've come to realise that many people interpret (or at least want to interpret) self-defence as a passive, non-aggressive act. They see self-defence as a magic amulet to be dusted off in times of crisis both to protect themselves from physical harm, and as a means to showcase philosophical opinions such as 'right is better than might' and 'weak can overpower strong', etc. Nice theories. Unfortunately, nice theories have nothing to do with surviving a non-sport, violent encounter.

Self-defence is ugly, and it is desperate.

It is a pressure situation where the risk of loss (of being injured) negatively affects the possibility of reward (survival).

As in any pressure situation, there are specific phases that require decisions and actions, which in turn influence the outcome and determine the result.

Understanding the anatomy of pressure is the first step to enhancing performance and, in the process, increasing your chances of survival.

The Three Phases of a Pressure Situation

Phase 1 is the *Error*.

This precedes all physical contact and relates to things such as bad planning, bad communication and bad choices. It can also include bad luck. Basically, you find yourself in a position or location that you shouldn't have put yourself in; you said or did something that you shouldn't have said or done.

Alternatively, you are simply unlucky and trouble finds you.

The essence of safety and security is to protect against the occurrence of *Error*.

In the world of close personal protection (bodyguarding), if everything is done as it should be done, the day-to-day functions of a bodyguard are spectacularly boring. There is nothing exciting about standing next to a VIP or President if you've done your homework beforehand — advanced reconnaissance, site inspections, route selections, guest vetting, maintaining appropriate skills like first-aid competency, etc. It's when you've slipped up in the preparation and planning stage or taken unnecessary risks that, in most cases, leads to something 'exciting' happening.

Personal protection should focus on identifying and defending against the occurrence of problems *before* they happen.

If you go to a red-light district by yourself, drink more alcohol than you can handle, stumble up to an ATM at two o'clock in the morning with your wallet in one hand and a cigarette in the other, don't complain the next day when you wake up in hospital, bruised, concussed and no longer in possession of your wallet.

Phase 2 is the *Bubble* of confusion.

The duration of this phase can vary considerably, from a few heartbeats to many minutes and in some cases even days or longer — but what is vital to recognise is that the progression from Phase 1 to Phase 2 is both linear and chronological. There is no 'past tense' in the *Bubble* — once you find yourself in the confusion of Phase 2, you can't go backwards and address the *Error* of Phase 1. To expand on the earlier example: if you are alone and drunk at an ATM in a red-light district when a predator chooses to mug you, you can't magically go back in time and undo the decisions and actions that resulted in your predicament.

Apart from the *Error* (or compound errors), which

invariably heralds Phase 2, common indicators of being in the *Bubble* are: denial, anger, frustration, blame shifting and wishful thinking.

All of these predictable human conditions are perfectly understandable, and completely useless!

Once you find yourself in the *Bubble* there is only one way to proceed, and that is forward! The more time you waste hoping the problem will magically disappear or wishing that someone else will fix it for you, the less chance you have of influencing the outcome in a way that serves you — not your opponent.

It is vital to appreciate the fact that action beats reaction. This is not a variable. It is a constant. Action beats reaction, *every single time*.

Regardless of the details of the *Error* that preceded Phase 2, whoever or whatever initiates an action once Phase 2 has been reached will *always* have a physical, a psychological and a combative advantage over their opponent. There are no exceptions to this.

Once the *Error* has happened, if you wait to respond to your competitor's actions and, in the process, allow them to 'pop' the *Bubble*, your inaction will dramatically undermine your chances of survival.

Conversely, if you initiate an action that bridges the gap between Phase 2 and Phase 3, you will force your opponent to have to respond to you. Even if the overall situation isn't desirable, it is always desirable for your opponent to respond to you — rather than the other way around.

To return to the example of the red-light district at two o'clock in the morning: once you find yourself confronted by a predator demanding your wallet, there *will* be a bubble of confusion as you try to figure out what's happening and subconsciously hope it's all a dream. The longer you wait and do nothing, the greater the likelihood that the predator will 'pop' the *Bubble* by physically assaulting you. Acknowledging that your decisions and actions that contributed to the *Error* were simply stupid, the outcome does not have to be physically painful.

The smart thing to do is to pre-empt the predator's physical assault by *voluntarily* handing over your wallet. Of course, I realise some testosterone-charged knuckle-heads will find advice such as this repugnant but, in the circumstances described, it is the best way to bridge the gap from Phase 2 to Phase 3.

Phase 3 is the *Result,* the sum total, of the *Error* of Phase 1 plus the action(s) of Phase 2.

The *Result* is more usefully viewed as 'more desirable' or 'less desirable' than as 'good' or 'bad'. Voluntarily handing your wallet over to a predator is not 'good', but it is more desirable than being beaten and hospitalised and in the process having your wallet forcibly taken from you.

In appreciating the consistencies of a pressure situation, it is also important to appreciate that making the transition from Phase 1 through to Phase 3 is pivotal to survival.

Of course, bridging the gap is difficult.

The fear inherent in the *Bubble* can easily transmute into indecision and procrastination which, in turn, can become like an irresistible drug. Indecision and procrastination are dangerous at the best of times. In a violent encounter they can cost you far more than a wallet or a bruised ego.

If you want to survive a physical assault, it is imperative that *you* initiate the transition from Phase 2 to Phase 3.

If the thought of doing so intimidates you (and if it doesn't intimidate you, you are probably suffering from unconscious incompetence or arrogant over-confidence) go back and revisit the two rules of self-defence*.

Also, give serious thought to how you can prevent the error from happening in the first place.

*1) avoidance and 2) survival.

2

Fear

FOR REASONS that are beyond me there are instructors, gurus and other experts who refuse to talk about fear. They'll talk about plenty of other things, such as qualifications, trophies, certificates and ivory-towered philosophies, but they won't talk about fear. Occasionally they may pay lip-service to fear by using acronyms such as *FEAR (False Evidence Appearing Real)*, which of course is utter rubbish. If I put my hand on a hot stove and burn my palm and then go to place my other hand on the same hot stove, the warnings my mind and body will scream at me are not *False Evidence Appearing Real*.

Fear is a vital part of our survival mechanism. It exists to keep us alive.

Failure to acknowledge fear in a regulated learning environment actually prepares us for failure in an unregulated, pressure situation.

Anyone who intends to survive a violent encounter — and that means bridging the gap from Phase 2 to Phase 3 — must understand what fear is and how it works. Failure to do so will result in failure to survive. This is as true for a martial art Black Belt as it is for a complete novice. And, as for the 'gurus' who are so skilled and so tough as to be fearless, they are either lying or stupid. Or both.

The following characteristics of fear apply not only to the realities of a violent encounter, but to any pressure situation where there is a risk of loss and a possibility of reward. Some of these characteristics are desirable, some are not. Either way, they are all part of what it is to be human.

Fear Is Natural

If you find yourself in arctic conditions with inadequate clothing, you *will* start to shiver. It doesn't matter how many tattoos you have or how many bar fights you've been in: if you are cold you will shake and, in the process, your vital organs will receive more blood flow than your extremities.

Similarly, if you are in the tropics and you are hot you *will* start to sweat; if you *don't* sweat, then you are in serious trouble. It's the same with fear; it's not an 'optional extra' for weak and cowardly people. Fear is a natural part of our survival mechanism. Live with it.

Fear Is Reliable

Unlike sporting competitions where there are fixed parameters, a violent encounter has far too many variables to accurately predict things such as the date and time of the encounter, the number of opponents involved, the weapons used, etc. One thing you can count on though is the presence of fear. In the face of perceived or actual violence you *will* be scared. Leave your ego out of it.

Accept the fact that you'll be scared and work with it.

Fear Mobilises

Some of the changes that occur in a pressure situation include: clammy palms, shaking knees, dry mouth, a loss of peripheral vision, auditory exclusion and, in more extreme situations, a loss of bladder and bowel control.

You also become physically stronger, physically faster and your pain tolerance level increases — sometimes dramatically. The way these changes are interpreted will vary from person to person (or perhaps more accurately, from ego to ego), but the fundamental purpose of these changes is to mobilise you for *action*.

Fear Constrains

Fear constrains body movement. Your ability to employ fine motor skills deteriorates in direct proportion to the perceived risk of loss. Putting a key in a lock, for example, is a simple neuromuscular coordination exercise.

There is nothing to it. The 'technique' of holding the key and inserting it into a keyhole is about as simple as you can get. However, when there is a violent risk of loss involved (let's say you have to open your car door to escape from someone who is intent on causing you serious harm) your ability to employ the 'technique' deteriorates.

Fear Inhibits

In the US the phone number to dial in an emergency is 911. In Britain it is 999. In Australia it is 000. Each country has simple three-digit numbers.

Imagine how difficult it would be to call an ambulance if your child was suffering a severe asthma attack and the numbers required were the same length as an overseas telephone number. You need to acknowledge that your ability to recall data in a pressure situation deteriorates because fear inhibits mental and physical coordination.

Fear Filters

Before you read the next sentence, take a moment to notice the feel of the jacket of this book and also pay particular attention to the type font used on this page.

You could have noticed those things a few moments ago (and on a subliminal level you did), but previously the data wasn't important and your mind filtered the detail out. That filtering process happens all the time and, in a pressure situation, the degree of filtering increases in direct proportion to the risk at hand. If the pressure is great enough you can become deaf, you can become blind, you can become impervious to pain.

Fear Distorts

In a non-pressure situation, time is a like a liquid substance; you can move it around from one container to another, splash some on the floor, drink some if you like and still the *amount* of liquid won't change. All that changes is the container.

In a pressure situation, time becomes like a gaseous substance: it can expand or it can contract — slow down or speed up — depending on the scenario. The same phenomenon of distortion applies to shape, size, quantity and colour whenever fear is present.

Fear Is Contagious

Fear is like a viral or a bacterial infection. It is contagious. Once one fear-related thought enters your mind, another will quickly follow. If other people are nearby, they too will start to be influenced by your fear — just as you can be infected by theirs. Channelling and directing this reality is a part of surviving a pressure situation and will be discussed in more detail in subsequent chapters.

Fear Is Proof

Whenever you experience fear — which is, among other things, a natural and reliable component of any pressure situation — there is almost always a buffer zone between the *recognition* of the threat and the *experience* of the threat. That buffer zone is usually proof that 'it' hasn't happened yet.

Understanding this has considerable value because (a) it focuses your attention on something that is important to you and (b) it indicates there is still some time to influence the outcome.

Fear Is an Opportunity

Of all the desirable and less desirable characteristics of fear, the most empowering is that fear is an opportunity — an opportunity to influence the outcome of something you have identified as important. The greater the fear, the greater the opportunity.

Let's say I'm out walking with my youngest daughter when a large dog attacks her — actually rips into her. I *want* that situation to have a massive impact on me because this is a major opportunity for me to influence the outcome of something that's important to me. That doesn't mean I want the situation to happen of course, but I do want to fully recognise that this is a situation that demands my total focus and complete attention. The last thing I want is a resting pulse rate of 52 beats per minute as I coolly try to disengage my child from the jaws of a violent dog. I *want* my heart rate to spike up to 200+ beats per minute. I *want* to stop thinking about irrelevancies such as when my car registration is due. I *want* a massive hit of adrenaline to charge my muscles, make me stronger and increase my pain tolerance level. If the cost of that adrenaline includes losing control of my bladder and bowels, then so be it! My ego can wrestle with those details later.

Right now I need to bridge the gap between the *Error* and the *Result* — and how well I do that is going to depend on my *actions* in the *Bubble*. If I stand by crying 'This can't be happening!', 'Whose dog is this?' or 'Someone call the police!' I'm squandering irreplaceable time.

Self-Defence in

3

Confidence

AS A professional speaker I stand up in front of many audiences each year. The demographics of those audiences vary considerably, as do the industries they represent, but what is consistent is that the response of each audience is predictable. If I ask an audience — be it twenty people or two hundred — to come up with a collective definition of confidence, invariably those definitions will include words to the effect that confidence is 'believing in yourself' and/or 'believing in your ability to do something'. Mmm, maybe. Maybe not.

If I believe, really *believe*, that I can fly (unaided) and I go to the top of the tallest building in my nearest city and stand on the roof of that building with total confidence in my ability to fly — well, my chances of flying remain extremely slim. And if I look down from that lofty height without a shadow of doubt or a flicker of fear and then leap out from my perch, my *belief* — no matter how strong — is not going to stop me from looking like a very large pizza when I hit the ground.

If confidence is the *belief* that you can do something, I think confidence is seriously overrated. If, however, confidence is the *capacity* to employ skill and knowledge when it counts — *even when you are scared!* — then I think confidence is perhaps the single most important characteristic needed to bridge the gap between the *Error* and the *Result*.

When you find yourself in the *Bubble* of confusion, it takes confidence to initiate an action that will carry you forward to the *Result*. Confidence, like so many things in life, is a choice. You can choose to procrastinate and hope the problem will go away, or you can choose to take advantage of the fact that positive action overrides negative thought. And you can choose to invest in the development of confidence long before the occurrence of any *Error*. Making that investment is arguably one of the wisest available to you.

There are five ways to develop confidence.

1. Experience the Characteristics of Fear
2. Develop Knowledge
3. Develop Familiarity
4. Develop Health and Fitness
5. Work Beyond Yourself

Experience the Characteristics of Fear

In a real test of stamina you can't fake endurance. It's the same with confidence. In a real test, you can't fake your capacity to employ skill and knowledge. If you want to increase your chances of surviving a violent encounter, you need to experience the realities of physical fear *before* you are faced with a potentially life-threatening situation.

Before you experience the *Error* — let alone the *Bubble* — you need to know in advance how *you* process and respond to fear. You need to deliberately and purposefully take part in activities where you are physically and psychologically stretched. Preferably it should be in something that intimidates you before you take part, but which you feel proud of having done once it is over. The specific details of what you do are of secondary importance; what matters is that you experience some type of stress that is not normally a part of your life.

If, for example, you have extensive experience in rock climbing and abseiling, you won't really be stretching yourself if you try some other activity that involves heights, such as parachuting or bungee jumping. If, however, you are a champion rock climber who has a fear of speaking in public, then do a public speaking course and deliberately seek out opportunities (make them if you have to!) to speak in public. This is how you improve. This is how you grow. And in doing so, you develop a type of residual strength you can draw on when you find yourself in the *Bubble*.

Develop Knowledge

There's a famous etching by the great Spanish artist Goya

titled *The Sleep of Reason Produces Monsters*, which depicts a man slumped at his desk while strange, bird-like apparitions flutter above his head. While the sleep of reason may indeed create fearful monsters in our minds, it is knowledge and reason that dispels them. Information shines the harsh light of truth on the subject of a person's fear and destroys its mystique.

Whatever it is that you don't feel confident about, make an effort to learn everything you can about it. Go on-line, get books from the library, buy trade journals, watch documentaries and videos. Seek out experienced leaders in the field and ask them questions, listen to them, learn from them. The more knowledge you gain, the more confident you will become.

It doesn't matter what the subject is, you can and you will improve your capacity to take part in the activity if you invest in learning more about it.

The subject need have nothing to do with self-defence: developing knowledge has a direct link to overall self-esteem, which is irrevocably linked with confidence in general.

Develop Familiarity

Familiarity delivers confidence. It doesn't matter whether it's driving a car, using a keyboard or wrestling, the more you experience something the more you understand it and, consequently, the less it will intimidate you. If you want to develop confidence — which is to say, increase your capacity to employ skill and knowledge in a pressure situation when it counts — you need to invest in developing familiarity.

When seeking familiarity with a subject, a good guide is to approach it as you would an exercise routine; start off slowly, develop a foundation and build from there. By developing familiarity you are moving beyond your zone of comfort. By definition, this means that the experience is going to challenge you. It's the challenge you need. Don't make the mistake of interpreting your discomfort — which is actually your growth — as proof that you should not be taking part in whatever it is that is challenging you. Like the ad says: Just do it.

Develop Health and Fitness

In addition to being a defence against many forms of preventable illness, the rewards of improving your health and fitness are substantial: enhanced mental capacity, focus and memory retention, an improved physical appearance, better sleep patterns and increased wellbeing. All of these improvements contribute to increased levels of self-esteem and personal confidence.

Confidence shares similarities with attributes like flexibility and aerobic capacity — it develops with training and it deteriorates with neglect. So does self-discipline. Regular exercise strengthens the body, relaxes the mind and toughens the spirit. Denying yourself simple pleasures, such as a glass of wine after an evening meal, may seem unnecessarily Spartan (especially in a society where more than half the population is overweight), but each small act of self-discipline fosters a will that can deliver unexpected strength in times of need.

Work Beyond Yourself

There are very distinct boundaries and equally distinct limitations to personal confidence when it is driven solely by thoughts of personal reward. That's not to say you can't achieve a lot if your motivating force is you. But if you go beyond yourself and work in a way that broadens your peripheral vision, so to speak, you tap into a source of energy and strength that is simply unavailable if your ambitions are purely selfish. If you want to be truly confident, you need to work beyond yourself.

Whether you are motivated to perform well for your family, your team, your company, your country or the greater good, protect and nurture that outward perspective. It can be the deciding factor in moving forward from *Error* to *Result* and bursting the *Bubble* in between.

4

Defence Assumptions

ASSUMPTION IS one of those words some people love to hate, but assumptions have their place. If someone passes me a firearm and in doing so they say: 'Don't worry, it's not loaded,' I'll assume they don't know what they are talking about and that the weapon *is* loaded.

Whenever a weapon is fired off accidentally, the *Result* is irrevocably linked to the *Error* of failing to respectfully assume that the weapon was loaded.

Similarly, there are a number of errors commonly made when dealing with aggressive opponents. Just as you should assume that all weapons are loaded, it will aid your survival if you realise that assumptions are not always a bad thing.

In particular, make the following a part of your mindset.

1. Your Opponent Is Under an Influence
2. Your Opponent Is Armed
3. Your Opponent Has Supporters
4. Your Opponent Will Charge
5. You Are Being Filmed

Your Opponent Is Under an Influence

Don't expect your opponent to respond to reason and logic just because you believe you are right and they are wrong. Take it for granted that there is something stopping him from responding rationally. He may be drunk, stoned or simply stupid, or he may be upset because he lost his job that morning. His car may have been damaged in an accident or his cat run over by his neighbour. Whatever the reason, it doesn't really matter. The thing is, don't take their attitude — or the comments they make along the way — personally. Even if they go out of their way to make it personal, don't allow yourself to be upset or shocked when they start to rant and rave at you. Instead, interpret the ranting and raving as proof that they are struggling for control while you are readying for the transition from the *Error* to the *Result*.

Your Opponent Is Armed

A common thing people say when they fire a weapon off accidentally is: 'Oh, I didn't know it was loaded!' One of the first things someone thinks when they get stabbed or clubbed in a street fight is, 'Oh, I didn't know he had a weapon!' A firearm is always loaded. An opponent is always armed. If you are wrong in making these assumptions, that's a bonus. But if you choose not to make assumptions (because you believe assumption is the mother of all stuff-ups) then by default you are assuming they *don't* have a weapon. It is a dangerous error to assume your opponent doesn't have a weapon.

Your Opponent Has Supporters

Many predators hunt in packs. Regardless of your martial rank (or lack thereof), when engaged in an aggressive confrontation you must take it for granted that your opponent has supporters. Assume there is someone standing nearby and/or behind you who is going to step in and help *your opponent*, not you. The advantage of making this assumption is that by pre-supposing a worst-case scenario as soon as the *Error* occurs, you have already begun the psychological transition from the *Bubble* to the *Result*. In effect, your assumption is helping you to reduce the amount of time you spend in the confusion of Phase 2 of a pressure situation.

Your Opponent Will Charge

Only in sporting events and testosterone-charged 'one-on-one' competitions of manly fisticuffs do fights start with opponents standing in front of each other in an 'en garde' position. Real violence is nothing like this. Real violence has a build-up period of some type — it might be a yelling match, it might be a staring competition, or it might be a predator silently stalking its prey before pouncing. However, when the transition from build-up to physical contact takes place, that transition is invariably explosive. It is an error to think that you will receive sufficient notice to register the transition from build-up to contact. You probably won't. Once your opponent makes his decision to commit to the attack he will charge in with speed, aggression and surprise. Assume this as par for the course.

You Are Being Filmed

When you find yourself in the *Bubble* many things will encourage you to be drawn into procrastination and inaction. The fear of legal ramifications, for a start. In a litigious society this fear is clearly not *False Evidence Appearing Real*. However, if you live and breathe the first rule of self-defence — avoidance — you need never fear legal consequences. If, nevertheless, you find yourself in a position where you *are* compelled to defend yourself or someone you care about, then act under the assumption that you are being filmed — and that a copy of the film will make its way to the court room where your actions are going to be judged. This assumption acts as a type of mental break; it encourages you to do what's needed, but not excessively. And make the following key points a part of your tactical blueprint: legally you *are* entitled to use physical force to protect yourself against an unprovoked attack *and,* contrary to popular belief, *you do not have to wait for someone to injure you first before you act.*

Let me give you an example. If an assailant points a pistol at my wife's head and says with real conviction and overwhelming aggression: 'I'm going to pull this trigger and blow her brains out!', legally I *do not* have to wait for that person to pull the trigger before I respond physically. If I believe that person is telling the truth and as a result I use my own weapon to shoot them first, I *will* be charged with assault with a deadly weapon (maybe even murder) but, and this is an important BUT, being charged and being convicted are two very different things. Let's assume, for argument's sake, that the matter proceeds to court and it is proved that not only was my opponent's weapon unloaded, it was a plastic replica. Nevertheless, the crux of the matter rests in what I believed to be true *at the time of action*.

If I believe my wife's life is in peril then I am legally entitled to protect her — and I will.

Even if it is later established that certain details erroneously influenced my action (such as not knowing the gun was a fake), it is unlikely I'll be convicted. This isn't a loophole in the law. It is there for good reason and illustrates the fact that, legally, you do not have to wait for your opponent to bridge the gap between the *Bubble* and the *Result*. The same principle applies to using empty-hand force. If your opponent's body language and verbal language is screaming that they are about to assault you, you *do not* have to wait for them to injure you before you act physically and pre-emptively.

Self-Defence in

5

Your Options

TO MAKE an informed decision about anything, you need to know what your options are. Failure to appreciate your options is an error and will negatively impact on your ability to bridge the gap between *Bubble* and *Result*. And if you know what your options are *before* you find yourself in the *Bubble*, you do not have to waste valuable time trying to figure them out first; instead you can move straight on to *choosing* one of the options and begin to benefit from the fact that action beats reaction.

When faced with impending violence, you have six options. Whether you like it or not, these options are all you are left with if reason and logic have failed to neutralise the aggressive intentions of your opponent.

All six options involve analysing and accepting cost. If circumstances beyond your control eliminate one or more of the options then you will be compelled to choose from the remaining ones. But, regardless of whether you have the full six to select from or not, two very important questions remain: *which* option do you choose, and *when* do you employ it? I will come back to these questions when I have run through the options.

In the time that you have available to you (which may potentially be measured in heartbeats) you must try and weigh the cost of participation against non-participation.

All participation has a cost in one form or another, just as all non-participation carries a cost. It doesn't matter how fast you can swim, when you get into the water you are going to get wet. It's the same with physical violence.

Basically, you are damned if you do and damned if you don't. As such, you need to accept a leadership role and choose which cost is more desirable. Whatever you do, don't forfeit that choice by letting your assailant decide on your behalf.

1.   Ignore/Leave
2.   Comply
3.   Dominate
4.   Stun and Run
5.   Restrain
6.   Incapacitate

Ignore/Leave

The majority of violent encounters have a lead-up period of some kind. The mode of lead-up can vary considerably: the predator might be using threatening body language, verbal abuse (in person or over the phone, via a third party) or encroaching upon property. If you sense tension that could develop into violence, a reliably good option is to leave.

This is not cowardice. This is common sense. This is your first option when faced with violence.

Comply

As a single default strategy, compliance can be very dangerous because it means that no matter what costs are involved you passively submit.

However, there are cases when compliance may represent the most effective solution to a confrontation. It's a question of judgement. If you are faced with a potentially violent situation and for whatever reason you can't negotiate a non-physical solution or you are unable to leave the scene, the wisest, most appropriate course of action may in fact be to comply. Do what they want. If there seems a reasonable chance that complying will work, and if you think and feel the cost of non-compliance would be too great, then comply.

For example, if two assailants are demanding your wallet, then it's probably best to give it to them. If, however, two assailants are demanding your spouse, you'll have to choose another option.

Dominate

Predators can read a non-combative attitude. If you are not prepared to fight physically if attacked physically, a predator will read this attitude as an indication of weakness.

To defend against this, take control — of your thoughts and of the signals you communicate. Stand up and confront the predator. Make a scene if you need to. In doing so you will unbalance their opinion of you. Do this boldly, with a loud voice, a sharp tongue or even a humorous warning. Let your opponent know that you are *not* going to passively comply. Even if you don't feel bold, pretend you are! You'll be surprised at how well this can discourage an assailant.

Stun and Run

If circumstances dictate that you should get away as quickly and as decisively as possible, stun and then run! The 'stun' of this option is vital for success because you need to make your opponent experience a 'brain blink'. You need to do something that has them thinking, 'Hey! What the hell was that!?' When you follow this option, don't get lost in the minutiae of what some martial arts guru told you is technically correct — just do it! Slap his face, kick his shin or throw a drink in his face, then run. What matters is that you do *something*, either to injure him enough from following you or, at the very least, to give yourself a couple of yards head start.

Restrain

Of the six options, physically restraining your opponent (with some type of joint lock, jujitsu technique, etc) is the most difficult to achieve because it requires a high level of athletic fitness (physical strength, good balance, etc) and/or technical skill. However, if circumstances rule the other options out, and if you believe you've got what it takes to succeed, then go for it — and good luck.

A word of warning: despite the popularity of restraint and control techniques, too many instructors who teach these methods have little (if any!) real world understanding of how very difficult it is to physically restrain a genuinely hostile assailant. The perverse truth is that these techniques work best against non-resisting opponents — semi-compliant training partners and people who don't need physical persuasion in the first place! My recommendation is that unless you are doing *at least* four hours of hands-on restraint and control-technique training per week, you should avoid this option as you won't have the skill required to succeed. If you *must* restrain your opponent, you will dramatically improve your chances of survival if you inflict a 'brain blink' before attempting to apply the restraint itself.

Incapacitate

This is the last of the options because it is the last resort. You have been backed into a corner from which there is no escape. The cost of complying is too great. You cannot dominate your opponent. You know that stunning and running won't work and that you do not have an appropriate level of skill and athleticism to succeed with physical restraint and control techniques.

The time has come to incapacitate your opponent.

The actual mechanics of how you do this will depend on your training history, the needs of the situation and to a large extent your personality and character. Are you capable of gouging a man's eye out to stop him from assaulting your child? Or does the prospect of blinding someone override the welfare of your child?

The answer is something that only you know, and in all probability you won't know for certain until you are unfortunate enough to be in that situation.

Choosing the Right Option ...

When faced with violence you will choose one of the six options. If you fail to make a choice you are, in fact, making indecision your choice — and that's never a good choice! In some situations, some of these options will be unavailable to you. For example, if you are a passenger on a flight and something untoward happens you will not have the option of leaving — unless you happen to have a parachute tucked away in your carry-on luggage.

Choosing *which* option is relatively simple. Not relatively *easy*, but it is relatively simple: listen to your *intuition* (not to be confused with prejudice, pride or greed). Like assumption, intuition is one of those words some people love to hate, because intuition is an intangible, it can't be quantified in a concrete sense. But intuition does exist, and we have it for good reason. Like fear, it is part of our natural survival mechanism. Intuition helps us to stay alive. So, if your intuition says *run*, then *run*. But, if your intuition says: 'If I run my child will suffer', well then you need to choose another option — whether you like it or not. Don't expect the voice of intuition to be one hundred per cent clear cut. Often it is apparent only *after* the event has taken place — by which I mean that with hindsight you can recall the inner voice that was trying to attract your attention but which, because of the confusion of the *Bubble*, you ignored. However, you can develop your ability to listen to your intuition — by investing in the development of *confidence* (which includes deliberately experiencing the characteristics of fear). A good rule of thumb is: if in doubt, go with your gut feeling — even if that gut feeling calls for action that is unpalatable in the extreme.

... at the Right Time

As for *when* you employ your chosen option — the ideal moment to act is on *the movement before the movement*. Understanding the realities of a violent encounter includes understanding people — and that includes learning how to *read* people and your surroundings. Use your peripheral vision to be conscious of who is standing nearby and possible escape routes you can take if need be. Take notice of how your opponent is standing, how far away they are from you, where their hands are, what they are holding, etc. And take a moment to become mindful of indicators of combative intent: shuffling body weight from one foot to another, repeated swallowing, rapid eye movement, quick or shallow breathing and *the movement before the movement*.

Any action will almost always be preceded by another action. It might be a shift of the head, a blink of the eyes or a twitch of the shoulder, but invariably something happens *before* the predator makes the transition from possible force to actual violence. Train yourself to look for *the movement before the movement*. It might be the clenching of a fist, the reaching for a weapon or it might be the slamming of a glass before he stands up to slam you. And it is on *the movement before the movement* that you should aim to implement your selected option. If you decide to Ignore/Leave, do it as he slams his glass down. Say: 'I'm sorry, this isn't for me' and then leave! If Dominate is the option you choose, slam your hand down on the table and verbally take command as he goes to slam the glass down. The same principle applies to the other options of Comply, Stun and Run, Restrain and Incapacitate.

6

Assegai

ONCE YOUR opponent commits to injuring you, the distance between him and you will decrease — rapidly. Whether the encounter starts with an ambush, a strike, a push or a grab, once physical contact has been made something primeval clicks in and the vast majority of predators fixate on getting progressively closer and closer to their prey. Unless you are an exceptionally skilled athlete, it is highly unlikely you'll be able to stop this body-space invasion. So, don't fight it. Embrace it. Literarily, *embrace* it.

In Southern Africa during the 18th century, the Zulu warrior's assegai — a short spear — revolutionised warfare in that part of the world. Prior to the assegai, battles had been staged with bravado and protocol that involved throwing long spears at the maximum, and often beyond the maximum, effective range. In this way casualties were kept to a minimum, egos were placated and reputations were enhanced.

When the African king Shaka Zulu introduced the assegai, all that changed. In the hands of a committed individual, the assegai was used with devastating simplicity: the distance between opponents was closed rapidly and audaciously, and at a range that allowed simultaneous grabbing and stabbing, the assegai was used to quickly finish the encounter.

Anyone interested in surviving a non-sport violent encounter can benefit from understanding the application of the assegai, in particular the *simultaneous grabbing and stabbing* which, as a tactic, is devastatingly effective. The reason for this is that it doesn't conform with any standard methodology. Usually people who stab, stab. Similarly, people who grab, grab: just as people who strike, strike. Some martial art styles practise switching back and forth between grabbing and striking, but rarely do people train to do both *simultaneously*. Surprisingly, doing both simultaneously is no more difficult than doing them separately. In fact, it is easier.

Think about it: which requires greater eye-hand coordination: hitting a moving target from a distance or a semi-stationary one from close range?

Unlike restraint and control techniques (wrist locks, joint manipulation, etc), which generally require a high level of competency to use successfully, basic strikes are a more reliable method of self-defence for most people in a pressure situation.

The best way to employ striking techniques is to use them as if they were wrestling tools. Whether it is a palm strike, a knee strike, a closed fist or whatever, deliver strikes as you *simultaneously* grab your opponent swiftly and with commitment.

Of course, to achieve this requires practice (see Fighting Fit), *and* being able to employ techniques is just one component in the jigsaw of self-defence. But it is an important piece of the puzzle, just as understanding pressure, acknowledging fear, investing in confidence, respecting assumptions and knowing your options are all important pieces of surviving a non-sport violent encounter.

Subdue with Confidence

At all levels of nature, weak does not attack strong. A hyena will not hunt a lion *unless* the lion is sick, injured or outnumbered. Human predators are equally selective: they go for easy options. A steering-wheel lock will not stop a determined car thief, however, a steering-wheel lock will *deter* a car thief and encourage them to find an easier target.

Similarly, if you fail to make appropriate decisions and actions *before* the occurrence of the *Error,* you have actually invited trouble because your (justified) lack of confidence will be subtly projected in the way you walk, talk and carry yourself. If you have decided that investing in the development of confidence is not for you — and it doesn't take a great deal of intelligence to come up with acceptable excuses to justify laziness — then that is the same as deciding that if someone physically assaults you, you won't defend yourself.

Conversely, if you take the time needed to gain an

honest appreciation of what effective self-defence entails, you will communicate signals that will actively encourage a predator to leave you alone — and as Sun Tzu wrote over two thousand years ago:

'The supreme art of war is to subdue the enemy without fighting.'

7

The Four-Flow Cycle

IN THE heartbeats before a hostile confrontation becomes physical, and from the moment physical contact has been made, there are only four things you need to do to influence the *Result* in your favour.

1. Shift Balance
2. Shift Focus
3. Seize Opportunity
4. Compel Response

The *way* you do those four things can vary, but regardless of the setting — be it a train station, a phone booth, a shopping mall or wherever — the flow remains constant.

Shift Balance

Shifting balance is best achieved through non-compliance, and one of the best forms of non-compliance is movement. In the animal world, the most common response prey will employ when they realise they are under attack is movement. Whether it's a bird, a fish, a reptile or a mammal, the primary action-orientated response is to move. The rationale for this is universal: a moving target is harder to hit, hold, bite or throw.

An additional benefit of non-compliance is that you demonstrate you will not easily submit. There is enormous value in sending this message because it will unsettle your opponent's confidence.

Shift Focus

Shifting focus is done by causing pain or a distraction. In some cases the pain or distraction (in the form of a strike, a loud yell or throwing a drink into an aggressor's eyes, for instance) can be enough to end the encounter, however its purpose is not to finish, but rather to create a 'window of opportunity'. For example, if a predator attacks with a knife, their focus will be on the blade and their target. If the defender does something such as kick the assailant's kneecap, the focus of the aggressor will momentarily shift to the smashed knee. That shift in focus provides the 'window' for the defender to follow up and take control of the situation.

Seize the Opportunity

Seizing opportunity is, more than anything else, a matter of choice: the choice of being a participant, not a spectator. The SAS motto — *Who Dares Wins* — says it all.

Whatever you do, do not allow fear to permit indecision and procrastination.

Instead, *commit* to being a part of the solution. And keep in mind: just because you didn't ask for a problem, that doesn't entitle you not to deal with it.

Compel Response

Compelling response begins with step three in this Four-Flow Cycle. By being proactive, not reactive, the participant capitalises on the irrefutable combative fact that *action beats reaction*. Response is compelled by *not* fighting the aggressor in the way they want to fight you. If they grab, you strike. If they strike, you grab. If they go high, you go low. If they push, you pull.

To put it another way, don't box a boxer, don't wrestle a wrestler, don't kick a kicker. That's not to say you can't kick a boxer in the kneecap or drive your thumb into the eye socket of a wrestler, it just means you shouldn't try and compete on their level.

You are not there to prove you are a superior sportsman to your opponent; you are there to do what needs to be done in the shortest amount of time possible. Leave your ego out of the equation.

Ego doesn't matter. Survival does.

THE FOUR-FLOW CYCLE
© R.P REDENBACH 2007

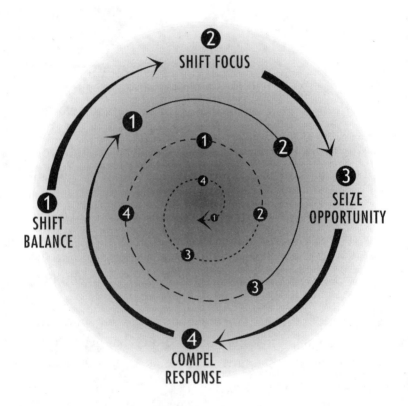

MOVEMENT IS UNCEASING

8

Pre-Contact

REGARDLESS OF your level of fitness or skill, it is possible to improve your chances of survival by employing the Four-Flow Cycle during the pre-contact stage when there is an escalation of tension but no physical contact involved.

Shift Balance

Do this by controlling your breathing.

As discussed in previous sections, fear is a reliable component of any pressure situation and, among other things, fear is a clamp that can tighten and restrict your capacity to do what needs to be done — when you need to do it.

A simple but extremely effective technique for relieving some of the pressure is to focus on the rhythmic movement of your lungs. In the confusion of the *Bubble*, some people do the exact opposite: they actually stop breathing altogether as the clamp of fear gets tighter. And as that clamp continues to tighten, their capacity to function continues to deteriorate.

Deliberately slowing down your breathing is as valuable as it is simple.

Don't get carried away or over-obvious when you do this, just avoid shallow, rapid breathing. Controlled, rhythmic breaths will reduce the physiological impact of a system going into overdrive in response to fear: by making your breaths deeper and emphasising slow, full exhalations, your pulse rate will drop.

This will in turn reduce (not eliminate, just reduce) the other associated symptoms of fear — such as shaking hands, clammy palms and dry mouth.

Shift Focus

Focus on your opponent's pain, not your own. Fear is a form of pain. Everyone feels pain in one form or another. Most people think about their own pain before they think about the pain of someone else. However, in the process of thinking about someone else's pain, you stop thinking about your own. Understanding this subtle fact has enormous value with broad application — not just in self-defence situations.

Often people who use the threat of violence (either implied or overt) are simply overconfident and underskilled. They practise bluff and brinkmanship more than they practise the development of real competency and, as a result, they project a confident exterior, but internally they are empty. As you stand in front of your opponent, reduce your own fear by reminding yourself that he has doubts and inadequacies. You might not know what they are, but he has them! Even when Mike Tyson was the undefeated heavyweight boxing champion of the world he stated:

'I definitely have fear every time I walk into the ring. I think that anyone who says they aren't scared is either lying or crazy.' And if they *are* crazy? Still tell yourself they have fear — even if it's not true, you are shifting your focus in a worthwhile way.

Seize the Opportunity

Choose an Option (review Chapter 5) and control the location of the fight, or at least control your location in the fight. Avoid an altercation on terrain of your opponent's choice because they'll probably be familiar with the area (which gives them an added form of knowledge and confidence). Take command of the confrontation and steer it to a site of your choice, not theirs.

For example, if a stranger tells you to get into their car, *do not* obey. Whether they threaten, plead, bribe or try to embarrass you in any way, *do not get into the car!* In this way you are demonstrating a degree of control over the situation by not passively accepting a subordinate role. It is a way of being a participant, not a spectator.

Compel Response

You can compel response by employing deception. The last thing you want to do is start a fight by saying: 'En garde, Sir!' Or even worse, adopting a formal martial art stance and saying: 'I must warn you, my good man — I am a Black Belt!' Apart from being ludicrously theatrical, this is a tactical error (unless you plan to use humour to disarm your opponent), because you are giving away one of the greatest combative weapons: surprise!

Always aim to take the initiative by employing a verbal or a physical deception to stun your opponent. And deceptions are only limited by your imagination: asking someone an unexpected question can act as a deception, as can doing something like putting your hands up in a position of surrender and saying: 'I don't want any trouble' before you kick them in the shin. The selection of the deception — along with the visualisation of a successful outcome — is an integral part of survival. It's simply a case of focusing on the *how to*, not the *what if*. The associated thought processes and visual images consistently override the debilitating side-effects of fear, while simultaneously allowing you to benefit from the combative fact that action beats reaction.

9

Weapon Defence

WHETHER YOUR assailant tries to strike you, grab you, stab you or club you, he is trying to use a weapon against you.

You will dramatically increase your chances of survival if you follow one defensive blueprint for all weapons rather than try to learn large repertoires of set responses for all possible variations. Again the Four-Flow Cycle can aid your survival, even if your assailant is stronger and more skilled than you are.

Shift Balance

If someone is trying to assault you with a weapon — regardless of the type of weapon they are using — do not be a stationary target. *Move!* The specific details of how you move are all secondary. What matters most is that you do not remain stationary. The importance of this cannot be overemphasised. Move and keep moving!

Having said that, don't let a philosophical preference — such as a reluctance to use physical force — stop you from doing anything else apart from moving. Movement

49

is a vitally important component of survival, but by itself it is not enough — you still need to Shift Focus, Seize the Opportunity and Compel Response.

Shift Focus

Shift focus by *striking*. When you strike, don't expect to deliver a knock-out punch — that can happen, but it takes quite a deal of skill (or luck). The purpose of a strike is primarily to provoke a 'brain blink' in your opponent, so that you can then take advantage of the following window of opportunity. However, it's important to realise that it takes energy and time to deliver strikes; they are like bullets in a fire fight, a finite resource, and to use them effectively you need to respect and abide by the economics of the battle.

Like many things, effective striking is about quality, not quantity. Madly flailing your limbs around like a windmill isn't really going to help you — and you'll be amazed at how quickly you become exhausted from doing that.

Whether you like it or not, to strike well takes practice.

The more complicated the strike, the more practice it requires (and because fear restricts and inhibits, the more complicated a strike is, the less chance you'll have of using it successfully in a pressure situation). Conversely, less complicated strikes, while still requiring practice, take less time to learn and maintain.

Thus, for your own sake, it is worth learning a compact skill base of uncomplicated strikes.

Seize the Opportunity

Seize the opportunity and *grab*. As previously discussed, once your opponent commits to injuring you, the distance between you will decrease rapidly. Unless you are an exceptionally skilled athlete, it is highly unlikely you'll be able to stop that body-space invasion. So, don't fight it; embrace it and, importantly, embrace it with aggression. In fact, take it one step further and tell yourself you are going to enjoy teaching the mongrel one hell of a lesson.

This last bit of advice may seem utterly ridiculous, but the prospect of enjoyment (no matter how small) enhances performance, and when combined with channelled aggression it can help override the negative impact of doubt. By directing your thoughts towards intense action you will capitalise on the fact that aggression is both an effective shield and a powerful offensive weapon.

Compel Response

You can compel a response by *changing* your technique every time pain is delivered or received. If you manage to grab your assailant, move on to some form of strike. If you punch or kick your assailant, follow up with a grab. In short, you keep following the Four-Flow Cycle. And remember, failure is also pain: so change on failure too. If you've tried to apply a specific skill (such as a restraint and control technique) and it didn't work, *don't* keep doggedly (more to the point, insanely!) trying to apply the same technique: change! The unpredictability of this approach, combined with genuine intensity, will allow you to use your defence skills to achieve better results.

And if you don't have any defence skills? Then just fight. Fight for someone you love, fight with commitment and do whatever comes naturally to you. If all you can manage is to bite your assailant's fingers off, then do that! And keep doing it until you have won the fight or you can't fight any more — or he runs out of fingers!

10

Ground Defence

AS DISCUSSED in Defence Assumptions, during a non-sport violent encounter you take it as a given that your opponent has supporters. Even if you are a judo Black Belt you cannot afford to *voluntarily* take the fight down on to the ground. It is tactical suicide to think that as you're applying some type of immobilisation technique (neck restraint, etc) your target's friends won't be busy caving your skull in. Again the Four-Flow Cycle provides the framework.

Shift Balance

Shift balance by resisting! It cannot be overemphasised how important, and powerful, non-compliance is once aggression has escalated to physical violence. Even if you have no skill whatsoever, when you *utterly refuse* to comply with the physical demands of an assailant it can be extraordinarily difficult for them to overpower you. Just as refusing to get into a stranger's car is better than complying and then later having to try and defend yourself in the back seat, so it is better to do everything you can to physically avoid a fight going to the ground. As hard as it can sometimes be to do this, you will at least *decrease* the possibility of a fight degenerating into a rolling match if *you* choose not to go to that level.

Shift Focus

Eyes–Fingers–Bite is the tactical reflex of gouging an eye, bending a finger and biting anything that's capable of being bitten *the moment* the fight goes to the ground.

The specific details of how an eye is gouged (with a thumb? with a finger?), which finger is bent or which part of their anatomy is bitten are all secondary.

What matters is that the assailant is forced to shift focus. The purpose of shifting focus with Eyes–Fingers–Bite is not solely to stop the fight there and then (although if that happens, well and good!).

The primary purpose of shifting focus is to create a window of opportunity to extricate yourself from the overly vulnerable position of trying to defend yourself from a prone position. Employ this strategy with genuine intensity, and remember that failure is pain. Change on pain. And changing on pain includes movement.

If you're struggling to locate targets: move!

Two things will happen when you do this.

First, the movement will make it harder for your opponent to gouge, bend or bite some part of you and second, by changing the spatial relations involved you will create new targets.

Seize the Opportunity

Make it your priority to stand up! In the same action of Eyes–Fingers–Bite, *simultaneously* make every effort to get up.

This is as much a mental imperative as it is a physical process: your heart must be screaming, 'Stand up! Stand up!' as your body scrambles to fill the gap the window of opportunity has provided.

As in any pressure situation where there is a risk of loss and a possibility of gain, whenever you are faced with an opportunity to influence the outcome of something that's important to you, you will experience doubt and apprehension. In the process you will be enticed to stay where you are — literally and figuratively.

Before that happens it is imperative you realise that if you want to control, or at the very least influence, the *Result* in your favour, it will come down to the actions *you* initiate.

Compel Response

Be different. Forget about trying to prove that you are technically or athletically better than your opponent. It is an expensive and unnecessary error to try and fight your opponent in the way they want to fight you. Don't trade techniques like two professionals in an exhibition match. If you come up against someone who has specialised in ground fighting — and that's why they want to take the fight to the ground — it is utter stupidity to try to fight them on their own level. Just as it is utter stupidity to try and out box a boxer or out kick a kicker.

Do what your opponent *doesn't* do. And in the process, don't get lost in irrelevancies of 'correct form' or 'style'. Focus on where you want to go, not on how you're going to get there. And whether you throw a technically correct reverse punch or a wild haymaker, do it with commitment — and no second thoughts! True commitment is very often the difference between winning and losing. Scottish philosopher William Murray was spot on when he wrote: *'The moment one definitely commits oneself, providence then moves too.'*

11

Multiple Defence

IF YOU are unfortunate enough to find yourself faced with multiple assailants, you need to seriously consider complying as your primary option. However, if the cost of complying is too great, then the following will assist in aiding your survival.

Of course, as with all defensive tactics there are no guarantees that you will prevail, but if you don't at least try, you have already lost.

Shift Balance

Shift balance by subtracting one — preferably the leader or the closest threat. Think of gang members as representing the legs of a table. If you remove one leg, you upset the overall 'balance'. Combatively, this is the outcome you want to achieve in a multiple defence situation.

The gang draws its strength from its collective presence. By unsettling its balance, you unsettle its strength.

In the heartbeats before the confrontation becomes physical or at the moment it becomes physical, aim to subtract one of the gang with some type of pre-emptive strike: raking their eyes, striking their kneecap, etc. This is a bold move — and necessary.

Whatever you do, make sure it has real impact. You don't get a second chance to make a good first impression.

As such, don't half-heartedly push one gang member in the chest and mumble: 'Um, okay, don't mess with me. Right?'

Shift Focus

Shift focus by shielding. The basic infantry tactic of engaging an enemy from an enfilade position (a flank or side angle) has been around for as long as there have been infantry soldiers. There is good reason for this: by fighting from a flank, you effectively shield yourself from your opponent's own support. By positioning yourself to one side, your assailant shields you from other gang members. To get to you, the support must get *past* the person you are engaging. Meanwhile, part of the attention of the person you are engaging is occupied with wondering something like: 'Huh? Where's my back-up?!'

Shielding is an effective way of shifting focus, and when used in conjunction with strikes you get a double impact. But remember, time and energy are finite resources and defending against two people isn't twice as hard as defending against one, it's more like three times as hard. In fact, the impact of multiple assailants is exponential.

As such, you really need to get serious and not just respond to opportunities — you have to make them!

Seize the Opportunity

Deliver a good skill — such as an elbow strike to the head, a finger jab to the eyes or a kick to the kneecap — on one person and then move straight on to the next attacker. If a leopard is attacked by a troop of baboons (and like human predators, baboons prefer to hunt in packs) the leopard will defend itself rapidly and audaciously by closing in on the closest baboon. At a range that allows simultaneous grabbing (with its jaws) and slashing (with its rear claws), it will disembowel its opponent with one swift motion of its hind legs. Without wasting time delivering multiple slashes on this first victim, the leopard will move straight on to the next nearest target. Follow the example of the leopard: deliver a good skill on one person and move straight on to another.

Compel Response

Move continually. Whatever you do, *don't* voluntarily become a stationary target by trying to emulate actors in a kung fu movie — deftly repelling would-be assailants as they politely enter your personal space zone one at a time. Force them to respond to you by being a moving target, and as you move keep looking for new targets to engage. And when you engage, aim to finish quickly!

It doesn't matter if your assailant starts with an ambush, uses a weapon, tries to take you to the ground, attacks in a group or does a combination of all these things: once physical contact has been made, it is imperative that you try to finish the encounter as quickly and decisively as possible.

The dynamics of real violence do not allow most people to last longer than 30 seconds in a non-sport affray. If it's some type of to-and-fro, push-me, shove-you yelling match, then yes, that can go on for *much* longer than 30 seconds. But push-me, shove-you yelling matches are garbage and you should just avoid them. They cannot be mistaken for a real confrontation that you can't simply ignore or walk away from. It is a tactical error to think you can be Muhammad Ali and win by slowly wearing down your opponent as you 'float like a butterfly and sting like a bee'.

If you must fight, then fight with intensity — a physical and a spiritual intensity. Get absolutely serious and embrace the chaos. Commit yourself to doing what has to be done as quickly and as decisively as possible, and in the process work beyond yourself. Think of someone who depends on you and who will be upset if you are hurt and then fight for them, not for yourself. If you do this, you will be amazed at the power you can tap into.

12

Fighting Fit

PHYSICAL VIOLENCE is, of course, violently physical. Astonishingly, some people seem oblivious to this fact. They want to believe utter garbage such as the myth that slotting keys in between fingers as a type of improvised knuckle-duster will keep a predator at bay and if, in a worst case scenario, force is involved it still won't involve blood or getting hurt. Such beliefs are prime examples of the *Errors* which precede the *Bubble* of confusion and which contribute to very expensive *Results*.

Regardless of your current level of physical strength, aerobic fitness, eye-hand-coordination, etc, if you *improve* those levels you will *improve* your ability to survive a physical assault. Better than that, you will actually *decrease* your chances of being chosen as a victim in the first place because predators favour easy targets — not fit ones. Of course, the extent of your improvement will be in direct proportion to the effort you invest. Don't make the error of doing nothing because you can't or won't match the training regime of an Olympic athlete.

As Shakespeare wrote: *'Nothing comes from doing nothing.'*

If you are currently doing nothing for your physical fitness, then it's relatively easier for you to improve than it is for someone who is already doing a lot. If you are heavily involved in training, I suggest you focus on *all* the jigsaw components listed here.

Either way, examples of how you can improve are given on the following pages.

The Jigsaw of Self-Defence

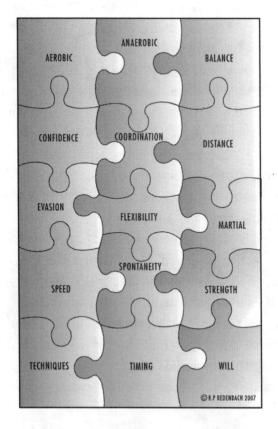

Aerobic

The better your aerobic fitness is, the more physically controlled you will be in a pressure situation and the less time you will need to recover from aerobic work. There are dozens of ways to improve aerobic fitness; the key is to choose the one you like the most (or the one you dislike the least!). Whether it's walking, running, cycling, swimming or rowing, try and do at least three aerobic sessions per week for a duration of at least twenty minutes. And remember, it's consistency and sticking with it that counts. You're better off doing just one session a week over a period of years, than madly doing six sessions a week for a few months and then none at all.

Anaerobic

The nature of a violent encounter makes it inevitable that at some point muscles will be used quickly and explosively. The by-product of this type of activity — lactic acid — is a painful fact of life for anyone who is forced to defend themselves against physical assault. Although it's not possible to stop the production of lactic acid, it is possible to minimise its psychological impact. You need to be familiar with the way lactic acid makes your body feel, the taste it puts in your mouth, the way it alters your breathing and the way it affects your balance and coordination. The way to do this is by performing any physical activity at a sprint pace for a solid 30 seconds

— it can be push-ups, sit-ups, skipping rope or sprinting upstairs: the details aren't as important as the intensity of application. Try and do this at least once a week.

Balance

Good balance is vital to surviving a violent encounter. You cannot afford to trip and fall just because the surface you are working on is uneven and different to what you are used to. With a little effort it is reasonably easy to improve balance. One simple way is to practise self-defence techniques with your eyes closed. This forces the inner ear and your body's other feedback mechanisms to adjust your position, rather than relying solely on your visual system to fix on a stationary object. By walking through your skill repertoire with your eyes closed you'll not only improve your balance, but you'll simultaneously improve your understanding of the skills. When you do this, it isn't necessary to spend hours every day on it. Just a few minutes will do.

Coordination

In the pressure of a violent encounter there won't be enough time to select responses by conscious thought. However, if you have a good working level of coordination, your ability to reflexively employ the appropriate skills will increase. To develop coordination, participate in activities where the outcome is not choreographed. Anything that involves eye-hand coordination and simultaneous footwork is particularly good. It doesn't matter whether it's squash, badminton or simply rebounding a ball against a brick wall, if it requires simultaneous foot movement, energy transfer and eye-hand coordination, it will help you.

Distance

If a person can do a flawless right cross, a spinning elbow strike, or whatever, but does not understand distance (the spatial relationship between their body and their opponent's), the skill will have no real value in a pressure situation for the simple reason that the person will not hit the target! However, someone who only knows how to do a swinging haymaker, but understands distance, will at least have the potential to hit the target — which of course is the fundamental objective of all strikes.

A simple method of developing your sense of distance is to train with a friend where you both use a bamboo stick or a piece of plastic pipe (about half an arm's length) to randomly strike at each other's legs and mid section — a bit like sword fighting. When you do this, don't worry about stances or techniques, just have some fun. Play with it, and learn in the process.

Evasion

The best way to avoid injuries and other consequences of a violent encounter is not to participate in a violent encounter at all. Preferable as this approach is, however, it's not always possible, although evasion — in the form of spontaneous movement — remains a valuable tool for avoiding your opponent's strikes, grabs and other weapons.

An effective way to develop evasive skill is to have a group of three or four people circle one person and try to simultaneously grab and strike that person.

The target can move in any direction he likes, but he is not allowed to strike back. The target's sole defence is to move and position himself on the flank in an enfilade position, thereby keeping the attackers in the way of each other.

As well as being excellent evasion training — not to mention aerobic, anaerobic and balance training — this exercise is great preparation for defending against multiple attackers.

And by developing the ability to outmanoeuvre multiple opponents, it will become progressively easier to outmanoeuvre a single opponent.

Flexibility

General flexibility is important for good health and wellbeing and is therefore of assistance in developing overall fitness. General flexibility does not mean you have to be able to imitate a ballet dancer (just as a ballet dancer will not, solely on the basis of his or her flexibility, operate effectively in an environment of aggression and violence). Invest some time in flexibility, but don't become preoccupied by it. Ten or fifteen minutes a day of stretching in conjunction with other exercise is a healthy addition to your lifestyle.

Martial

To better appreciate what it takes to defend yourself and the people you care about, it is worthwhile experiencing some martial arts training. The bad news is: there are many martial arts instructors with little or no honest appreciation of what effective self-defence entails — and they often don't know that they don't know. The good news is: there are many martial arts instructors who *do* understand what effective self-defence entails. How can you tell the difference? Experiment.

Go out and take part in at least one martial art training session … in twenty different styles! And then, and only then, choose the style you feel suits you best and take part in a further twenty sessions of that style. Next, decide if you want to stay with that style, move on to another or not train at all. If you choose the easy option and just try the two or three styles closest to where you live, you won't be doing yourself any favours. Even if you try a dozen different styles, it will not be enough. You really do need to experiment with *at least* twenty different styles. This may seem like an arbitrary figure, but in my experience the sheer variety of martial arts styles is in itself intimidating for many people. You need to minimise the intimidation factor by gaining familiarity.

And they need to be *different* styles. Don't just do twenty different kicking styles — try some wrestling, some mixed styles, and some traditional styles. Experiment. And, pay particular attention to the examples set by the instructors and the attitude of the people you train with. Even if you know next to nothing about martial arts, you do know something about people. Use that understanding to objectively evaluate what's going on around you. And don't be afraid to listen to your intuition: if something inside you says: 'Nope, this isn't for me' then let go and try another style. Conversely, if your intuition says 'Yes! This is it!' that's dandy … but, still go out and try twenty more styles before returning to the one you thought was best.

Speed

Just as strong people like to praise the virtues of strength, those who are naturally fast like to praise the virtues of speed. The fact is, both speed and strength have value. Focusing on one to the exclusion of the other will not provide the combative versatility required to survive a non-sport violent encounter. To develop an appropriate balance of speed and strength, start by thinking of the two attributes as variations of the one condition. Then seek out activities and exercises where you receive some type of instant feedback if you fail to employ enough speed. Anything that is done with a training partner (in contrast to an inanimate object) will have the added benefit of simultaneously increasing your competitive drive.

Spontaneity

Spontaneity is that almost magical quality of *flowing*. When you can flow from one movement to another without conscious thought, you don't need cartloads of techniques to be successful in a pressure situation. And an effective step towards flow and spontaneity is, ironically, *not* possessing cartloads of techniques. The more compact your skill base is, the easier it is to move from one element of it to another without deliberation. However, possessing a compact skill base requires *confidence*: confidence in the skills themselves and confidence in your ability to instil those skills as working reflexes. And, for another dash of irony, if you don't possess the confidence and discipline to instil a compact skill base as reflexive, you will not have the confidence and discipline needed to instil a large skill base as reflexive. It might seem like a closed circle, but you just have to break in at some point and the most reliable way of doing so is to focus on refining a compact skill base.

Strength

There are two forms of physical strength: inanimate strength and living strength. Inanimate strength is the ability to move non-living objects — to lift iron bars, for example. Inanimate strength can be very impressive and is easily quantified. Living strength is the ability to move and/or control non-cooperative living opponents. In a violent encounter, a history of inanimate strength development will aid your survival, however it is the living strength which is most often the difference between survival and loss.

A good living strength exercise is to have two people try to pull, drag and push one person from Point A to Point B, perhaps a distance of thirty metres. None of the parties is permitted to bite, gouge eyes, bend fingers or strike, but everyone involved must apply 100 per cent physical effort to the task at hand. The target resists, not by using formal techniques, but by internally screaming: *'I'm not moving!'*

Techniques

As previously discussed, basic strikes — in contrast to joint manipulation and other complicated techniques — are a more reliable method of self-defence for most people. How to make any strike its most effective is by concentrating and focusing your energy. When practising a strike:

1.   Close your mouth at the point of impact
2.   Tense your midsection
3.   Exhale through your nose and
4.   Hit *through* the target.

Accuracy — in the sense of actually hitting what you are aiming at — is very important, but don't get too preoccupied with hip angles, toe placement, body rotation, etc. As long as you focus on the weapon (that part of the body you are striking with) and *commit* to connecting with the target (bridge of nose, temple, etc), your body and your mind will work out the best way to transfer energy at the point of impact.

Practising strikes by hitting a punching bag or a focus mitt is always a good use of training time, but there are other ways to improve striking. Keep in mind that a strike is simply energy transfer — you are transferring energy (force) from your body into and through your target. Energy transfer is generated not so much by mass as by good body mechanics. To develop good body mechanics, participate in activities which involve concentration, leverage and balance. Anything where you are required to push, pull, throw or spin will do this. Even chopping wood with an axe will improve your ability to deliver strikes. And as with any exercise, make sure you balance the activity by working the left and the right sides of your body in equal proportion — and yes, that includes chopping wood!

Timing

Timing is similar to distance: without it your skills will not have any practical value. You need to be able to time the delivery of strikes, etc to coincide with the positioning of your target — if not, your strike won't connect. There are any number of exercises that will help you improve your sense of timing. Sparring with a training partner is one example: striking a light punching bag is another. In the long run, the best way for you to improve yourself is to incorporate your individuality into what you do and how you do it. It is the process of exploration and experimentation that is the real education of training and development.

Will

The will to win is the single most important component of survival. Unlike things such as muscle size, rank or financial status, a will to win is intangible. Even so, it can be developed. It's like a muscle to that extent. It develops with training and it deteriorates with neglect. Seek out activities which involve competition and demand focus. So long as the activities challenge your willpower, and so long as you perform them with genuine commitment, you will improve your desire to win. Whether you actually win in competitive sports doesn't matter — so long as you *try* to win.

In the stress and confusion of a pressure situation, it's not whether you *can* fight, but whether you *will* fight that matters. The will to fight is seeded long before you find yourself in the *Bubble*. The will to fight grows from all the collective decisions and actions which directly and indirectly influence your self-esteem. While it is possible to fool some of the people all of the time and all of the people some of the time, you cannot fool yourself. Just as the *Result* of a pressure situation is the sum total of the *Error* of Phase 1 plus the actions in the *Bubble* of Phase 2, so your opinion of yourself is the collective result of choices and actions you make on a day-by-day basis.

Self-Defence in

13

Train to Improve, Not to Impress

IN THE end, how you fare has as much to do with how you think and feel about yourself as it has to do with any martial skills you have accrued.

If you don't really believe you are worth anything then, sadly, there's a good chance that when push comes to shove, you'll simply comply, no matter what the cost.

But, the fact is, you *do* have an innate right to defend yourself and the people you care about. The question is, are you willing to *do* anything about it?

In all areas of life, achievers do what non-achievers can't be *bothered* doing.

Whether it's in the planning and preparation stage or in execution and follow through, very often the individuals and teams who gain superior outcomes are those who take the important steps along the way.

Most of those steps could be achieved by just about anyone: by themselves they are neither overly difficult nor spectacular. What matters is that each step — or jigsaw component of a larger mosaic — is made with genuine commitment.

The same principle applies to self-defence.

Once hostile aggression becomes physical violence, the bad news is you have, at best, 30 seconds to save yourself.

The good news is that those 30 seconds haven't happened yet. In reading this book you have improved your chances of survival because you have already done something positive *before* the occurrence of the *Error*.

You are currently in the buffer zone between the recognition of a problem and the experience of a problem. It's not too late. You have an opportunity to improve.

Start by reading this book a second time.

(Yes, I'm serious.)

Then, make a list of the things you can do to improve your chances of bridging the gap between the *Bubble* and the *Result*.

Once you have that list, go out and do what non-achievers can't be bothered doing.

Train to improve, not to impress.

R.R.

Recommended Reading

Art of Peace - Morihei Uyeshiba. (Shambala).
Art of War - Sun Tzu. (Shambala).
Book of Five Rings - Miyamoto Musashi.
Budo Karate of Mas Oyama - Cameron Quinn. (Coconut Productions).
Descriptive Study of Law Enforcement Officers Killed - Vaughn, JB & Kapperler, VE.
Karate-Do My Way of Life - Gichen Funokoshi. (Kodansha International).
Life Tips - Mark McKeon. (Courtney Ballantyne).
On Killing - Dave Grossman. (Little, Brown and Co).
The Naked Ape - Desmond Morris. (Vintage Books).
The OODA Loop - Col. John Boyd.
Waveman - Robert Redenbach. (Courtney Ballantyne).
Who Moved My Cheese? - Dr Spencer Johnson. (Vermilion).
Zen in The Martial Arts - Joe Hyams. (Bantam Books).

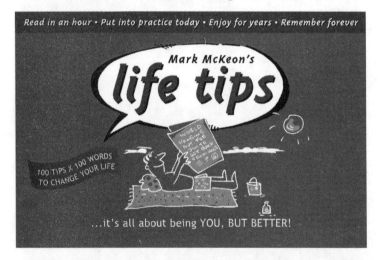

ALSO BY ROBERT REDENBACH

WAVEMAN

ISBN 9780646470399

"A tour de force!"
Peter FitzSimons – **Sydney Morning Herald**

"There is a philosophical depth to Waveman that goes well past the action and adventure, although you can read it on that level too. It's a great, inspiring and motivating read, with wider audience appeal than it would first seem."
Joanne Schoenwald – **The Westerner**

"Waveman is more than a bio – it's a life class in perseverance, ambition and ignoring convention, even when the odds are stacked against you."
Penthouse Magazine

"A page-turner, bursting with action and entertainment."
The West Australian

"Redenbach perfectly captures the events of one man's past to help others imagine and then strive for a better future."
Gold Coast Bulletin

"Pleasantly surprising . . . Redenbach displays wonderful attributes."
Alive Christian Magazine

"A great raging story that takes you to unlikely places all over the world. It's a wild ride!"
Richard Fidler – **ABC**

"The over-riding charm of Redenbach's autobiography is that despite the dangerous locations and his obvious skill, the author is self-effacing as he teases out the fibre of human integrity."
Jane Fynes-Clinton – **The Courier Mail**

Purchase a signed copy of *Waveman* direct from
www.redenbach.com